SUN BEFORE DEPARTURE

Fiction
Saturday Night and Sunday Morning
The Loneliness of the Long Distance Runner
The General
Key to the Door
The Ragman's Daughter
The Death of William Posters
A Tree on Fire
Guzman, Go Home
A Start in Life
Travels in Nihilon
Raw Material
Men, Women and Children
The Flame of Life
The Widower's Son
The Storyteller
The Second Chance and other stories
Her Victory
The Lost Flying Boat

Poetry
The Rats and Other Poems
A Falling Out of Love and Other Poems
Love in the Environs of Vorenezh
Storm and Other Poems
Snow on the North Side of Lucifer

Plays
All Citizens are Soldiers (with Ruth Fainlight)
Three Plays

Essays
Mountains and Caverns

For children
The City Adventures of Marmalade Jim
Big John and the Stars
The Incredible Fencing Fleas
Marmalade Jim on the Farm

SUN BEFORE DEPARTURE

Poems 1974 to 1982

ALAN SILLITOE

GRANADA
London Toronto Sydney New York

Granada Publishing Limited
8 Grafton Street, London W1X 3LA

Published by Granada Publishing 1984

Copyright © Alan Sillitoe 1984

British Library Cataloguing in Publication Data

Sillitoe, Alan
  Sun before departure.
  I. Title
  821'.914   PR6037.I55

ISBN 0–246–12305–2

Printed in Great Britain by
Richard Clay (The Chaucer Press) Ltd,
Bungay, Suffolk

Contents

PART TWO: POEMS ON THE THEME OF ISRAEL

Acknowledgements

Ambit
Bernard Stone for *Poems from Israel* with drawings by Ralph
  Steadman, Steam Press, 1982
European Judaism
Festival 1981 (Colchester)
Grass (Australia)
Harrap Anthology
Here and Now (Terence Kelly)
Jewish Chronicle
Jewish Quarterly
Leonard Baskin's Press
Ma'ariv (Israel: translated into Hebrew by Moshe Dor)
Nottingham Quarterly
OUP Anthology
Outposts (Howard Sergeant)
Pacific Quarterly
Poetry London-Apple
Sceptre Press, Martin Booth
Shepway Writers Anthology, South East Arts, 1982
Strands, Adam Feinstein
Times Literary Supplement
Topographical Essays and Poems, Ronald Blythe, OUP
Words Broadsheet, Julian Nangle

Part One

SUN BEFORE DEPARTURE

Geographers in Love

Surveying is a scientific art
And love an artful science,
But geographers in love use both
On their reconnaissance.

A base-line laid precisely down
Is traced through chin and navel,
And checked repeatedly for error
In your land and mine.

We chart, and shape
The contours of each cheek.
Shadows show spot-heighted bodies
Layer-tinted, and eyelashes hachured.

Geographers in love
Triangulate every minor feature –
And amorously note
All data in a fresh revision;

With subtle accuracy ply
Hills and valleys of each traverse,
Closing point to point
In mutual compassion.

The clashing of tectonic plates
In loving solids and artistic drift
Makes the features on our map
Impossible for science to improve.

Topography's volcanic fuse
Engraves a map where only Death
Can sign the final sheet
And leave no date.

Horse on Wenlock Edge

A tired horse treads
The moonpocked face
Of a half-ploughed field;

Cuts furrows blindly
Through drifting rainfall
On chestnut trees and soaked grass.

Energy diminishing with evening wind:
Seven nails in each steel shoe
Are empty scars of twenty-eight nights

In which the white horse dreams
Of galloping through star-clouds to the moon,
A month of nails stampeding from its path.

Nottingham Castle

Clouds love floodwater, play with
Distorted shekels between grass
Enriched by the tips. The city flattens
All surrounding land with rubbish.
From the Castle Top
Binoculars ring the distance like a gun.
On serrated roofscape left and right
Churches lift and chimneys lurch
Above a sea of shining slate.
Towers and modern blocks block visions.
'The Robin Hoods' drilled up and down
And practised azimuths on far-off points,
Eyes watering at southern hills
A half-day's march away:
'They'll have to swim the bloody Trent,
God damn their goldfish eyes!'

Musket balls rush, break glass,
Make rammel. The Nottingham Lambs
Did more damage than a foreign army,
Came up through twitchells
And set rafters sparking,
Painted pillars with the soot of anarchy.
The sly Trent rippled in the scarlet night,
Too far off to douse the fires out.

The council got our Castle – finally,
A museum stonily protected
By Captain Albert Ball V.C.
Who thrust into a cloud-heap above Loos
Hoping for his forty-second 'kill'.

In school they said: 'You're born
So that Captain Ball has someone
To remember him. Otherwise he'd die.'

A private soldier turned into Icarus:
'Dearest Folks, I'm back again
In my old hut. My garden's fine.
This morning I went up, attacked five Huns
Above the line. Got one and forced two down,
But had to run, my ammunition gone.
Came back OK. Two hits on my machine.'
Fate changed him to a concrete man
With an angel overlooking
On the lawn of Nottingham's squat fort.

Memory takes a flying leap:
There were barges on the Leen before my time,
A fleet of sail tunnelling my heart,
Each a slice of paper with Life's writing
Packed in a script of tunic-red.
Forty years ago I blocked the view
Bemused no sudden push came hard enough.

Another brain shot down in sleep:
Rich Master Robin Hood – outside the walls
Where he belongs – robs me of time
But keeps it for himself and not the poor.
The whimsical statue stood
With hat and Sherwood weapons
Till a Nottingham Lamb sneaked up and stole his arrow
(Someone later took the bow)
Before Death with its sonic boom
Blew sunlight through the horizon's window.

I leave a ghost near the black wall,
As Little John tolls every quarter-hour,
A dream in the darkest boxes of the night
Stifled beyond my eyes.
The hills that sleep fall with me
To clock hammers flattening minutes
That never speak in the same voice.

Oxney

Smoke all evening, too thin to move.
The stubble was aflame
Up a hillside when I drove
Across the flat half-mile between

Iden and the Isle of Oxney. A line
Of white lipped in red set a corner
Of the battlefield on fire,
And cloud like a grey cloak was pulled along

By some heart-broken mourner going home.

North Star Rocket

At the North Pole everywhere is south.
Turn where you will
Polaris in eternal zenith
Studs the world's roof.

Under that ceiling
A grey rocket pencils
Across a continent of ice,
Evading earth by flirting with it.

Who will know what planet he escaped from?
A cone of cosmic ash pursued its course
On automatic pilot set to earth

Bringing Death – or a new direction
To be fed into its brain
Before collision.

Fifth Avenue

A man plays bagpipes on Fifth Avenue.
Gaelic wail stabbing at passersby
Who wish its pliant savagery would
Draw them through their fence of discontent
To a field of freedom they can die in.
They stand, and then walk on.

A man with thick grey beard
Goes wild between traffic,
Arms like wagging semaphore;
Raves warnings clear and loud
To those ignoring him.
Dying isn't important any more.

A blind man rattles a money-can,
Dog flat between his legs
Listens to the demanding
Tin that has so little in
Both ears register
Each bit that falls.

An ambulance on a corner:
They put a man on to a stretcher
Who wants air. A woman says:
'Is it a heart attack?
Is the poor man dead?'
She worries for him.
Dying is important when it comes.

11

'I suppose it is,' I guess.
'I hope it's not too late' –
She had one last year:
'Fell in the street – just like that.'
Her lips move with fear.
The man spins into a stroke.
He's slid into the van.
Dying, a lot of it goes on.

Just like that.
Easy come and awful go
For the bagpipe player in the snow
The wild man with his traffic sport
The old man with his dog
And the not so young who hurry
Wondering why the journey has to stop.

Picnic

The bigger the river the vaster the ruin.
The ocean does not notice.
Waters move and countermove
And the ruin is rebuilt.

The smaller the stream
The fouler the dream;
Ocean does not notice
Nor the sky.

Ruin changes and the ruin stands.
The curtain of the sky draws to.
The river runs
The ruin glows.

I reflect –
Eating bread and olives
On the stones.

Stones in Picardy

Names fade on stones: the suave
Air of Picardy erodes
The regimental badge or cross
Or David's Star
Of Gunner This and Private That.
The chosen captains and their bombardiers
And those long known as nothing but to God
Who brought them out of slime and clay
Are taken back again.

God knew each before they knew themselves
(If they ever did)
Before mothers' lips sang to them,
Brothers showed
Sisters taught
Fathers put them out to school or work.
But only God may know them when the stones are gone,
If any can –
If God remembers what God once had done.

The Lady of Bapaume

There was a lady of Bapaume
Whose eyes were colourless and dead –
Until the falling sun turned red;
Her lovers from across the foam
Walked at dawn towards her bed
But fell in fields and sunken lanes
And died in chalk dust far from home,

A rash of scattered poppy stains.
Nowadays they pass her wide –
That mistress of *chevaux-de-frise*
Is still alive and can't conceal
Her mournful and erotic zeal:
The lady of Bapaume had charms –
Bosom large, but minus arms.

No soldiers rise these days and go
Towards the bloodshot indigo.
Motorways veer by the place
On which, with neither love nor grace,
They drive to holidays in Spain.
There was a lady of Bapaume
Whose lovers ate the wind and rain.

August

Birth the first attack
Begins at dawn.
Also it's the last, whistle at sun-blood
Illogical, unsynchronised, inept.
Children pushed over the top
And drummed across churned furrows
Kitted out with dreams and instinct
Hope to learn before reaching the horizon.
Those in front send back advice:
'I'm going to advance, send reinforcements.'
But who trust the old when they as young
Spurned cautionary wisdom
That never harmonised with youth?
'I'm going to a dance, send three-and-fourpence.'

Some fall quietly
Under each rabid burst of shell
Love of life unnoticed in
Willingness to give it
Or the feckless letting-go.
Autumn leaves drop
In the zero-hour of spring
Young heat called suicide
When mangled by motorbike or car
At the dead end of a shadowed valley.

Broken sight looks inward
No view beyond.
Though dust is entrailed
And terror rocks the heart to sleep
The signalling sky sends words:

Get up, look outside, it's day again.
Insight is blinded by energy
And warped by innocence.

The battlefield widens. Bullets rage
At friends and parents.
Strangers don't count,
Stunned in the lime-pits of oblivion.
Who blame for this sublime attack?
Don't ask. Ask if you will.
Did Brigadier-General God
In his safe bunker plan?
He horsebacks by.
Wild cheers. Choleric face knows
Too much to know. To tell
Us would be dangerous
For any smile to live.
Whoever is cursed must be believed in.
Baal is dead. Get up. Push on.
Want to live forever?
Go through. No psychic wound can split
Or leg be lost at that onrushing slope.

Half-way, more craven, sometimes too clever
Old campaigners want a hole to flatten in
Before brain-rot encircles,
Or Death's concealed artillery
Plucks hands from the final parapet.
Silence kills more quickly
You can bet. Live on:
Death pulls others in
Not you, or me, or us (not yet).

Earth underfoot is kind but waiting,
Green sea flows on the right flank,
Black rain foils the leftward sun,
Poppy clouds and mustard fields
Tricked out with dead ground, full woods,
Lateral valleys flecked with cornflowers.
Roses flake their fleshy petals down.
Time falls away. Battle deceptively recedes,
Peace lulls to the final killing ground,
Familiar voices coming up behind.

Terrorist

The protest is against death.
The raised fist, the face
Of corruption bewails its declining
Gift of life. I will go when chosen for taking.
The sky bruises the aching fist. Air mellows
The corroded face. You did not choose me.
I parted myself long ago when I sat
On a tree-branch overlooking boathouse
And bulrushes, and the lake water
On which nothing moved
Except the breath of words
Saying no seven times all told.
I didn't stay to hear
The answer yes or no:
Turned and ran blind into Death's donkey-circle
Till the rag around my fist
Was bloodsoaked from hitting trees.

Rabbit

A busy rabbit,
albeit young and small,
cornered our vegetable plot.
How it did, we'll never know.

Chewing green treasure,
going with upright tail
from line to line
in rabbit-fashion –
whose all-providing God laid out
row on row of grub,
it scarpered back to thistles on mornings
to lie low till heavy-treading
vengeance went away.

The fur-lined malefactor
was resolved on lettuce, carrots and peas
at which he'd fed for a fortnight,
sly enough to keep the news
from his myriad friends below.

A heavy pellet in the gun,
I stalked that gorging salad engine
whose tender paws on soil
sensed the extra weight
of pellets in my pocket –
and soft-footed off before I reached the hedge.

Next morning my shadow
a mere half-way across the lawn,
he heard his blackout coming up,
odds low on lead-slug
batting its head before my final chop
against the too well-padded neck.

It never happened –
though if that produce had been all
between hunger,
my senses would have sharpened
and the gun become God Almighty.

Moth

Drawn by the eyeless glitter of a lamp
A slickwinged silver moth got in
My midnight study and ran quick
Around the switches of a radio.

Antennae searched the compact powerpacks
And built-in aerials, feet on metal paused
At words like METER-SELECT, MINIMUM-MAX
TUNER, VOLUME, TONE
Licked up shortwave stations on to neat
Click-buttons with precision feet.

Unable to let go the next examination
My own small private moth seemed all
Transistor-drunk on fellow-feeling,
A voluptuous discovery pulled
From some far bigger life.

A thin and minuscule antenna
Felt memory backtuning as it crawled
Familiar mechanism, remembering an instrument
Once cherished in its world,
Forgotten but still loved for old-times' sake.

I switched the wireless on, and the moth
To prove it had a better bargain
Mocked me with open wings and circled the light,
Making its own theatre, which outran all music.

Fishes

Fishes never change their habits:
A million years seem like a day
As far as fishes' habits go.

Beware of those who change them half as fast
Like people every year or so
So fast you cannot find a grain
Settled firm in eye or limb.

The constancy of fishes is unique.
They multiply, but keep their habits
In deep and solitary state.

They feel unique and all alone
Not being touched and hardly touching
Even to keep the species spreading –
Unique in never-changing habits.

Fishes are flexible and fit the water,
And though continually moving
Never change their habits.

Thistles

Dry thistles in summer
Grow in spite of flowers spreading;
Brittle taproots draw succour
Till next autumn.

Sickly thistle seeds flop from the hedge,
Past puberty suck their fill
By beans and carrots.

Entrenching blade hacks soil,
Fingers under spikes grip
And easily out it comes
Tossed to the sun's bake.

The useless thistle pricks fingers
That gather and inflate with pus.
All year long
The hand aches in memory.

Release

Flowers wilt. Leaves are feloniously snatched,
Birds sucked away. Autumn happens.
Frenetic bluebottles saw the air.
Blackberries scratch with poison when you reach.

Love is grabbed before knowing the mistake.
The last thief grins
And takes the gift of life.
There are so many, who cares?

The trap is a loaded crossbow,
Ratchet-pulley sinewed back
From birth and set in wait.
None walks upright from the bolt's release.

Wood near Wittersham

A tractor on the curving lane
Pulls a wagon-load of children
Going fishing to the river,
Leaves a silence we can
Be alone in and hold hands.

You look at stubble burning
I stare into the wood.

We choose between a future seared
Or a past before the fire spread
And danger sheltered us.

When we turn for home
Open field and dark wood
Share possession of our shackled love.

Lefthanded

The left hand guards my life.
I use. It uses. Sinister
Alliances shape plans.

Left hand is fed by the heart
Strategically engined
Between brain and fingers
Sometimes filtering intelligence.

The left eye is in line with hand
And pen. The left lung
Rotted when I tried the right hand.
Lesson One was spitting blood.

A lefthand friend makes puppets walk
Respects long union
Tolerates no break.

Vulnerable left side lives in harmony
And liberates the rules,
Rides monsters who fear to eat themselves
So do not bite.

Illness

An illness is like a pearl dropped in wine
It breaks the spirit and softens the body
With an accelerating express ticket
To the endless tunnel.

Some lay down to die
Then after sleeping deny what was heard
As hope crushes the will.

Others do it better, and quickly
In case the trickery of indecision
Outlasts the fatal shock.

Thoughts blown clear by the wind
Create a life-affirming drill
That pulls the sky behind,
Spiralling to break out.

To the New Moon

Since men have walked on her
Waved flags
Classified geology with peacock colours
Sent cameras probing every angle
The moon has turned Lesbian.

Good luck to her.
She shows brighter
In her woman-hunger
Burns with a purpose

As she looks for a lover
In the Milky Way or
Equally futile
Waits for one from Earth.

But better by far
Than shining palely,
Or full and bloody:

A mirror for courtiers to gawp at,
And stricken poets who ached
In her unrequiting light.

Chasing the Dead

Chasing the dead
They didn't move.
Ghosts are real, but dead.
Hands worked and could not catch
Shadows in his head.

Chasing the dead at night
They ate his dreams,
Ghosts craving to be fed
On their pursuers.
Ghosts live off dreams
Feast at night on what comes their way.
He neither woke, nor left off dreaming.

In daytime he thinks
Of chasing the dead, sunlight
Embellishing the feast for night.
Can't disentangle sinews
But pursues continually
Whoever waits but won't be found,
Until they eat him.

On First Going into a Factory to Work

Looking in, the sky's shut off.
Hard to tell whether Heaven is inside
Or the other place.
You can't judge by the smell.
In life you're either sitting safe
With legs between the railings,
Or your head's stuck firm and can't twist free.
If all that's good is good
The trio beckoning is stench
And noise and dazzle.

Lights illuminate each knight
Bent at a machine whose bulk
Runs wild within instead of out.
Intensity is lavished on each
Concrete-bolted steed
Worked with arm-pulls
Flash of spinning knuckles
Creased brows, steady feet
And shrewd eyes.

A pal three weeks already there
Carries a medallion grin
As if a decade presses on his neck –
Glance asquint and fag in pocket
Overalls with archipelagos of oil
Ears closed to noise that pushes
What is human to the walls.

There's glory in machinery
As each sniffs the odour
Like a war-horse its gunpowder.
Tell me another, except
Give us this day our daily sweat
And weekly pay. The clock looks on
At limbs you never knew you'd got.

The only choice is to wallow
In the drill and cut of work.
Or walk out. Machinery
Decides the spirit
That will break or stay.
Like Castor and Pollux
Heaven and Hell
Were born on the same day.

Suicide

As on a rolling wartime upland
Good men and better women
Fall left and right
From scorching shrapnel.
Their own hands fight
In enfilade to do the deed

Who cannot wait for flu to strike
A car smash or kidneys to pack in –
So many ways to choose.
Comes down to one dull breakthrough
Better than shameful deliquescence.
But compassion sucks survivors dry.

Car Dump

Cars piled high
in hills and vales of motors
which no one can deny
were one-time extraordinary floaters
whose tin rooftops glinted at the sky.

All were loved like dogs, or dragons,
petted, fed and washed, or polished;
now a drop of metal in an ocean –
more like bedsteads than fast wagons
with no memory of shape or motion.

A car that passes by won't look
in case a sharp ferocious hook
should pull it in and pound it thin;
or before, on a straight bit roaring off,
it's stricken by a fatal cough.

Nor do drivers care to view
such headstone-radiators beckon,
but rush through traffic lights on BLUE
to where they think sly years won't reckon
the wearing out of flesh and metal.

Death

Ophelia lay a finger on the water.
The cold and shallow brook
Scorched flesh. She pulled it back.

The fire was love.
She was forget-me-not's daughter
Each eye a pond of flowers.

If all was seen, no corpse
Came drifting from the weeds
As in poems, canvases or plays.

She climbed the arching cliff
Where water burst its clouds of salt
Like flowers across the sun.

The nunnery was found:
No one saw her body spin.
A lunar sea-change sent it cleanly in.

The Fate of an Icicle

An unthinking icicle
riding a bicycle
went too close to the sun –

singing a song
a newly-born icicle
went to a place
where he didn't belong –

a newly-born icicle
pedalling a bicycle
thoughtlessly
singing his song of the frost
went too close to the sun
and got lost.

Whatever he felt
as he started to melt
he soon fought free of the flame –

which sent back the bicycle
minus its icicle,
propelled by the power

of a thundery shower.

Optics

Better to see the earth
from a star
than peer as if at
a cockroach in a jar.

Binocular landscape
at 5-mile range
is scratched in sharp detail
and set beyond change.

To observe from a mountain
or cumulus sky
gives Godlike proportion
to the sacred eye.

Likewise the past
viewed from present terrain
reshuffles confusion
and makes patterns plain.

I'm part of that country
which filters the senses,
when the shape of its soil
leaps through the lenses.

Near speaks to far
and far answers near,
harmony forming
and meaning more clear.

Between the unseen and seen
mind's optics descend,
machine of perception
in space without end.

Space Dividers

Brass and steel perfection
of navigational dividers
measure havoc
between absconding planets.

Two points calculate
split distances
within which nothing stood
and space was gone.

But open bifurcating arms
and touch two points –
well-spanned yet lost forever
in curvatures of unity.

Age

I wonder –
When I'm old
Bald
Without teeth
Wanting breath
Almost blind
All loving finished,
Neither girl or woman
To kiss anymore
Or be kissed –

Whether poetry
Will come better
Recalling
The memory of storms.

Alioth

(A star from the constellation
of Ursa Major)

A bigot walks fast.
Get out of the way
Or walk faster.

He walked faster too
Veered right
To evade me.

I increased my rate
Hinging left to avoid
The fire of his eyes.

Collisionable material
Should never promenade
On the same street.

We muttered sorry
But went
More speedily than ever.

41

Lucifer's Bridge

Lucifer, fallen from grace,
Seeks the sun with his southern face.

A bridge on the journey south
Crosses a rivermouth.
Avoid the peril of a boat.

Boatmen on the north shore
Paper walls with placard warnings
That the bridge might crash.

They gloat at his dilemma but –
Am I dying? was his only question.

Changing Course

Down the slope to the horizon
Fix the black-dot sun before departure.
When the day sets at the storm's end
Far along the moonbeams that flow in,
Shut the barometer, hang the watch away
Lay the sextant in its box.

How deep the valley which enclosed
The lifeboat washed against the shore.
The heart bursts when it says
Goodnight at dawn,
And hopes the dark is best
Which fears the day to come.

Part Two

POEMS ON THE THEME
OF ISRAEL

On First Seeing Jerusalem

The only way to knowing is to know
how useless it is
to talk of hills and colours
while looking at Jerusalem.

One knows, and so keeps silent:
yet in keeping silent
one no longer knows.

But one never can unknow what was known,
not let such silence
drown the heart.

One knows. One always knows;
refuses to believe that silence
is a better way of knowing.

One sees Jerusalem and knows,
yet does not know. One comes to life
and feels that walls outlast whoever watches.

The Temple was destroyed: one knows for sure.
One joins the multitude and grieves.
One knows it from within.

One does not know. Let me see you
every day as if for the first time
then maybe I'll know more:

which must already have been said
by wanderers who, on coming home,
regret the loss of that first vision.

The dust that knew it once is mute.
The stones that know it all
stay warm and silent.

The hills are dry, but pale enough
to let me watch Jerusalem
and for a while make silence with the stones:
an ever-new arrival.

Nails

Tel Aviv is built on sand:
sand spills from a broken paving-stone
and sandals cannot tread it back;

waves beat threateningly
up the shore;
a sea to flow through traffic
climb hills and wash Jerusalem.

Every white-eyed speckle of its salt
feasts on oranges and people
as if envying their safety;

and their rock through which
six million nails have been hammered
as deep as the world's middle
and the sky
flood-tides can't reach.

Coast near Nahariya

The sea is like electro-chemical salt,
Rippleless tinplate lit this morning
By the sun that knows its place.
A distant cape is a grey chicken foot
Splayed under its own low roll of cloud.
It may be raining over there
But here a cooling peace is on the shore
That smells of oranges from narrow terracing.
Such coolness in this latitude
Makes silence easier to hear. The shimmering
Tin-lit sea moulds in its violence.
What moves in me moves under water,
Secret storms impossible
To sling my leaden heart into and read
The knotted fathoms when I haul it back.
Sky and sea are dull as air
Where no liquid colour flows,
But for the bluest fish-eye ringed with speckled
Brown and hemmed by panic as it flits through
Oceans shouldering each other, too quick
To see except in storms beneath
Unsilvered mirrors. So I turn
Back to you as, year by fathomless year,
The feeding of our love goes on
From the smell of oranges and ancient sources.

Learning Hebrew

With coloured pens and pencils
And a child's alphabet book
I laboriously draw
Each Hebrew letter side by side
From right to left
And hook to foot.
The *lamed*, narrow at the top
And then quite wide,
Sets the steel pen deftly thickening
As it descends
And turns three bends
To make a black cascade of hair,
Halting at the vowel-stone
And stepping-point to one more letter.

A page of script comes up like music
To bless life and the first blue of the sea,
Or the season's ripe fruit
And the act of eating bread:
They look like songs
Each sign a new born soul
Hewn out of flesh and rock
By hands that wanted God as well as Beauty.

I'm slow to learn except these letters
With cloud-tail shapes and whale-heads
Arks and ships in black, pure black, the black
Of the enormous sky from where they came,
Behind a wall of flesh and rock.

With their surety and law
Such unutterable shapes
Make me once more illiterate
And hurt the heart
As if the sky is bruising it:
Struck blind I'd go on drawing
In enlightened darkness
To stop a boulder bigger than the earth
From crushing me.

Such help I need
When lost in this slow writing,
Clutch at a letter like a walking-stick
That sets me tapping
Into the *samech* cavern-mouth where,
Though afraid of sleep, I curl up
By a phosphorescent letter
Asking if it's *aleph* or *tav*
Beginning or end
Or the lit-up middle.

Dreams dissolve
Yet when light comes back
The blind hand still writes
Hebrew letters cut in my rock
And painted by a child on the page.
For they are me, and I am one of them
But don't know which.

Synagogue in Prague

The killers said before they killed:
'Death is the way to Freedom,'
But seventy-seven thousand names
Carved into these great walls
Make a prison that no death can open.

Legs walk, fingers touch
Eyelids close in awe and sorrow:
That name was my mother
That boy starved to death, my son
Those men gassed – my brothers
Those who died of typhus
Are my oppressed and striving cousins.

It might have been me and if it was me
Where is my name?
I spend all day searching the words
For my name.
I'd be glad it was not me
If they could look again at the sky,
Reach that far-off river and swim freely in it.

What can one say
That was not screamed at the time?
Shouting rots the brain. The dead god
Hanging in churches
Whose followers through centuries have kept it going
Will never hear –
Yet such Man's work calls for revenge
To ease the pain of having let it happen,
To stop it being planned again.

Huge crimson letters of revenge
Daubed on such a wall
Would vandalise that mute synagogue,
And the seventy-seven thousand names
So stonily indented
Would still show through.

Vengeance is Jehovah's own.
To prove He's not abandoned us
He gave the gift of memory:
The Fruit of all Trees
In the Land of Israel.

For a Jewish Prisoner in Russia

When prisons get hungry
they find us.
Jailers search fog or sunshine
with carbolic breath.
There's always someone willing.

Bigmouthed prisons feed a tyrant's belly
eat the blameless and unlucky
for speaking doing or merely being.
A drawbridge of steel teeth
clamps jaws tight.

Puppet-fingers tug the strings
till inmates grimace
at the rattle-walk of jailers.

Prison holds the flesh but not the spirit:
senses are trodden to a voice
that goes beyond barbed wire or iron bars,
scatters broadcast
to all bloodstreams tuned to hear.

A single innocent inside
Like Samson rocks the tyrant's empire.

An Old Friend Reaching Jerusalem

Don't ask what I am doing here:
olive-leaves on one side glisten tin
the other is opaque like my dulled hair.
I travelled far. I walked. I ate
the train's black smoke
and choked on Europe's bitter sin.

The gathering of molecules goes on.
Forests rose from falling ash.
I gleaned the broken letters of my alphabet
and sucked them back to life for bread.
I scoured every hectare clean.

Christian roofs were painted red.
In Poland all the trees grew salt.
Marshes swallowed moon and sun:
four horizons slammed their doors.

In Russia hands still chafe
at livid scars that never leave.
Khmelnitzki's gangs of long-ago spared none:
seven hundred Jewish villages were razed
and now a city bears his name.
Infamy is honoured in that place.

My soul once honed by Europe's earth
and pulled apart by Europe's sky
is polished by Jerusalem:
compass-points may darken
but I still walk the city
and fall fearlessly in love,

stand ashen by the Western Wall
and through my tears no one dare ask
what I am doing here.

Festival

The moon came up over Jerusalem
blood red.
An hour later it was white,
bled to death.

The breath of memory revives
on the Fifteenth Day of Ab.
The spirit and the flesh
don't clash when men and women
walk in orange groves
to reinvigorate the moon.

God knew the left hand
and the right
when Lot chose
the Plain of Ha-Yarden
and Abram – Canaan.

An excruciating noise of car brakes
comes from the Valley of Hinnom.
Jerusalem is ours.

The Sea of Galilee (Yam Kinneret)

Galilee is a lake of reasonable size,
unless immensity is measured down
in dreams, in darkness.
Then it becomes an ocean.

Distant sails are like birds trapped
on its unreflecting surface,
single wings showing
as if savage fish below
chew at their heads and hearts.

With such casual intensity
and such immensity
are new dreams made from old.

Vision

The Dead Sea lives
as white birds fly
through chemical disturbance
from Samaria to Moab.

Magnetic landmarks
give cross-bearings
from Mount Nebo and Masada.

White birds fly on turbulence
from Moab to Samaria
navigating by
Masada and Mount Nebo

to build their nests
on one shore, then the other.

Ezekiel

On the fifth day
in the fourth month
of the thirtieth year
among the captives by the river
a stormy wind came out of the north.
Ezekiel the priest
saw visions:

    Saw Israel
    had four faces
    four wings
    four faces:

        the face of a man
        the face of a lion
        the face of an ox
        the face of an eagle.

That was the vision of Ezekiel.

The Rock

Moses drew water from a cliff.
I set my cup
till it was filled.

Water saved me, and I drank,
reflecting on
the shape of flame

of how a fire needs putting down
by swords of water,
always winning, never won.

On the Last Soldier Killed in the War of Independence for Israel, 1948-9

When it is the greatest luxury to forget,
the dead pay. They pay for everything.
The javelin of death has parted
them from breath and rain.

Each of that six thousand dead
who died rebuilding Zion
was told this by a thousand
from that previous six million:

'Memory is taken from the dead to give
eternal peace that life denied.
It is the living who remember,
for whom the Book must never close.'

Israel

Israel is light and mountain
bedrock and river
sand-dunes and gardens,
earth so enriched
it can be seen from
the middle of the sun.

Without Israel
would be
the pain
of God struck from the universe
and the soul falling
endlessly through night.

Israel
guards the Sabbath-candle of the world
a storm-light marking
Job's Inn – open to all –
an ark without lifeboats
on land's vast ocean.

Aleph

There are some people in the world
who do not even recognise
the Hebrew letter 'Aleph'.

God, look kindly on them.
Their night is all-enclosing.
But the stars shine through.

In Israel, Driving to the Dead Sea

I drive a car. Cars don't
figure very much in poems.
Poets do not like them,
which is strange to me.

Poets do not make cars
and they never have, not
one nut or bit of plexiglass
passes through their fingers.

No reason why they should.
To make a bolt or screw
is not poetic. To fit a window:
is that necessary?

Likewise an engine.
It makes a noise. It smells,
and runs you off too fast.
What's more you have to sit

as fixed at work as that
poor engine-slave who made it.
Nevertheless, I drive a car
with pleasure. It makes my life poetic

I float along and tame
the road against all laws
of nature. I stay alive.
Who says a poet shouldn't drive –

on a highway which descends so low
yet climbs so high
from Jerusalem to Jericho?

The Dead Sea Talk of Two Tourists, near Sedom in Israel

As the Red Sea is not exactly crimson
Nor the North Sea very far north
Nor the White Sea, by any standards, clean
Nor the Black Sea dark, or even coloured
Nor the Pacific unreasonably peaceful –
Neither is the Dead Sea deceased,
She said to him – in so many words.

Yet it is different, he replied in just as many,
Not because it is hot or cold
Or deep (in fact it's shallower than most.
He was filled with general knowledge)
But because its walls are closer
To the middle of the earth than any other
And therefore to me.

The Dead-asphaltic-Sea, she said
Is often called the Sea of Lot.
Mineral salt and chemicals
Make the water nauseous and bitter.
Fresh eggs and the human body float on it.
Organic life is not completely lacking
Which can, I suppose, be said of you as well.

I've also read books on the matter, he replied.
Each day the Jordan pours
Six million tons of water in,
A vast amount which totally evaporates
Due to heat and the sea's high walls.

And so the bitterness remains forever.
To swim in it is difficult, well nigh impossible.

That may be why you can't see underwater, she rejoined.
When you opened your eyes to try – remember? –
Twin flames burned the middle out of you, as well I know,
And fires likewise assailed those open cuts
Never noticed when you got them,
Reminding me of that perimeter
Your flesh can't push beyond.

It doesn't need to. The Dead Sea kindly floats
The living meat that loves my bones;
Outriding hands and rudder feet
Keep me flat and in a pose where I
Observe the sky that hardly changes,
Yet feel the fundamental pull
That holds me like a magnet to the water.

If one can call it such, she said.
At least you'll never drown in it.
Mutual unwillingness to see the other's point of view
Even when they're the same (especially then)
Left them floating naked on their backs
At midday under the Dead Sea sun in summer,
Buoyant and unalterable, burning to a cinder.

Ein Gedi

(After Shirley Kaufman's essay
'The Poet and Place')

If it matters whether to go or stay
What bleeds more?
When David went, the itch of death
Was in the air. The Salt Sea
Bloomed. King Saul bit himself
And followed. The cave
Had no windows to steam
The view. David's gloom was
David's soul, and hid him.

Whether to go or stay became
A cloak that fitted when he went.
After the mournful grackle's note
Saul came searching
But never felt the sword that cut
His cloak. Darkness is our place.
The cave gave David birth:
Memory was born from it
And so were songs.

Eve

In Israel one day
I looked out of a window
And saw Eve.

Her hair was so black
I called her Midnight
But no answer came.

Her eyes were amber
Jewels from the midday sky
When she looked at me.

She crossed Gehenna
In her sandals.
My daylight wanted her.

That few-minute love-affair
Lasted forever
When she went into her City.